Woodland Whispers
Owl Beanie, Scarf
&
Fingerless Glove Set

by

Janis Frank

Table of Contents

Within these pages, you'll discover a delightful collection of knitting patterns that blend the warmth of traditional knitwear with the whimsy of our feathered friends, the owls. Whether you're a seasoned knitter or recently conquered the fundamentals along your crafting journey, this book offers something special for everyone.

This trio of patterns infuses charm and personality into your winter wardrobe essentials: fingerless gloves, a snug beanie, and a classic scarf, each adorned with the captivating allure of owls.

These designs are more than just garments; they're a celebration of the artistry and joy that knitting brings into our lives. As you embark on your knitting adventure, immerse yourself in the rhythmic dance of stitches, and watch as these whimsical owls come to life, stitch by stitch.

So gather your needles, select your yarn, and let your creativity take flight as you embark on this cozy journey through the world of knitting and owls.

Happy knitting!

Knit Flat
Owl Beanie or Toque

This is a fairly easy project to make if you have some knitting experience. I designed it to be flat, knit on 2 straight needles so more people would be comfortable in making it. Though the cabling can look intimidating, it really isn't. I have videos on YouTube that will show you how if you've never done it before. I added both links and QR codes so you can easily find the videos. Either click the link (as you already know) or use your phone or tablet to take a photo of the QR code. A link pops up. When you tap the link, it goes directly to the video and starts playing.

The choice of colour is yours as always. I included where to change colours if you would like to make one with 3 colours like I did for the brown and beige version I made. If you're making a solid colour toque, you can ignore the notifications in the pattern.

As far as the use of a pom pom on the top... Some love it, some hate it. I know for myself, if I have to put my hood up, I hate them, but aesthetically, they do have their charms NGL. I have more information in the *Hints and Tips* section about the pom pom on the white and blue beanie.

Things You Need

Worsted weight yarn (either complimentary colours or single colour)

5 mm (Size 8 US) single pointed knitting needles

Cable needle

Tapestry needle to sew seams and work in ends

14 or 16 buttons or jewels for eyes (see Hints and Tips)

Pom pom – you can make or buy these, or not use one at all.

Gauge

In *stockinette*

9 sts = 2 inches (5 cm)

12 rows = 2 inches (5 cm)

Sizes are written as such:

S-M (L-XL)

Small and medium = 21 inches (53 cm) around

Large and Extra large = 24.5 inches (62 cm) around

Uses about 160 meters or 180 yards. Does NOT include pom-pom.

This pattern makes either 7 or 8 owls around. Each owl motif is about 3.5 inches (8.9 cm) wide if you follow the gauge given. You can adjust your stitches accordingly to make larger or smaller sizes than what I've given. Each owl motif uses 12 stitches. So, if you wanted it smaller by one owl cast on 74 sts (86 – 12 = 74)

The Pattern

Cast on 86 (98) sts

♠ **Row 1:** Knit

Row 2: Purl ♠ Repeat from ♠ to ♠ for a total of 10 rows. (*Change colour at the* **START** *of row* **11** *if desired.*)

To save yourself time if you're changing colours, I suggest that you Work in the Ends While Knitting. or scan the QR code below to learn how.

Row 11-15: Knit (*Change colour at the* **START** *of row* **15** *if desired.*)

Row 16: ♦ P2 K1 P8 K1 ♦ Repeat from ♦ to ♦ until there are 2 sts. P2

Row 17: ♣ K3 C4B C4F K1 ♣ Repeat from ♣ to ♣ to the last 2 sts. K2

If you are uncertain how to make the C4B or C4F, you can use the QR codes below:

C4F

C4B

Row 18: ♥ P2 K1 P2 K4 P2 K1 ♥ Repeat from ♥ to ♥ to the last 2 sts. P2

Row 19: K5 ☺ P4 K8 ☺ Repeat from ☺ to ☺ 5 (6) times more. P4 K5

Row 20: As row 18

Row 21: As row 19

Row 22: As row 18

Row 23: As row 19

Row 24: As row 18

Row 25: As row 19

Row 26: As row 18

Row 27: ♣ K3 C4B C4F K1 ♣ Repeat from ♣ to ♣ to the last 2 sts. K2

Row 28: ♦ P2 K1 P8 K1 ♦ Repeat from ♦ to ♦ until there are 2 sts. P2.

Row 29: Knit

Row 30: As row 28

Row 31: Knit

Row 32: As row 28

Row 33: Knit

Row 34: As row 28

Row 35: ♣ K3 C4B C4F K1 ♣ Repeat from ♣ to ♣ to the last 2 sts. K2

Row 36: as row 28 (*Change colour at the **START** of row **37** if desired.*)

Row 37 – 40: Knit (*Change colour at the **START** of row **41** if desired.*)

▲ **Row 41:** Knit

Row 42: ◘ P2 K1 ◘ Repeat from ◘ to ◘ tot he last 2 sts. P2 ▲ Repeat from ▲ to ▲ for a total

of 22 (26) rows.

Next row: ♣ K2tog K1 ♣ Repeat from ♣ to ♣ to the last 2 sts. K2tog

Next row: ◘ P1 K1 ◘ Repeat from ◘ to ◘ to the last st. P1

Next row: K2tog to the end of the row.

Next row: P across

Next row: K2tog to the last st. K1

Next row: P across

Break yarn and draw through. Sew the seam using the blanket stitch. Add a pom-pom to the top if you like.

Hints and Tips

I used repurposed yarn for the pom pom on the white toque with the blue banding. Unraveling the slippers I had originally made, it left the wool in the crinkly state that occurs. I haven't washed it so I don't know if the fluffy/fuzzy look will stay, but I certainly do like the effect it gave to the final pom pom.

If you are using multiple colours for your toque, I suggest you work in the ends while you knit. It saves you time in the long run. You can either click the link or take a photo of the QR code below to learn how.

Sew the seam using a blanket stitch to make it as invisible as possible. I added enough stitches along the sides so you can do this.

You can make the beanie fit closer to the crown of the head by not doing as many repeats of rows 41 and 42. You can also make it longer (taller and floppy) by doing more.

You can use whatever you like for eyes. Buttons will work. I used 8 mm flat back cabochons. They come in a variety of colours and sizes. I looked for more realistic owl eyes but all I could find were ones for taxidermy and they were too big, and expensive. I also recommend gluing them on as sewing will take a bit of time.

Take a photo of this square for more
FREE knitting patterns on my website!

Knitted
Owl Scarf

Owls seem to hold a draw for a lot of people, myself included. I think there are as many reasons as there are people as to why this happens.

You may be wondering why there is a seam to sew and why this isn't made in one piece. The owls look a bit different when you make cables from the top (head to feet) and from the bottom (feet to head).

Also, the band on the end needs to change from knit stitches (garter) to purl stitches. It's just all around more complicated than it needs to be. Besides, the seam is nearly invisible and less effort than going through the effort of trying to make the ends match if made in one piece. Trust me. I did try to make it one piece. I even wrote it down as I made it. One out of 10. Do not recommend.

Things You Need

Worsted weight yarn - either complimentary colours or single colour. How much depends on how long you want to make the scarf and if you want fringe.

5 mm (Size 8 US) single pointed knitting needles

4 mm (Size 6 US) single pointed needles (optional but strongly suggested)

Cable needle

Crochet hook (for fringe. Size doesn't matter as long as you can use it for yarn)

Tapestry needle to sew seam and work in ends

Gauge

In *stockinette*

9 sts = 2 inches (5 cm)

12 rows = 2 inches (5 cm)

Gauge isn't really important, but if you are making the beanie or hat to match, you'll want the gauge to be the same as the hat.

The scarf is one size fits all.

The Pattern

Cast on 40 sts with the 4 mm needles (you don't have to use the smaller needles but it helps keep the starting edge from splaying out wider than the scarf).

♠ **Row 1:** Knit (If using the smaller size needles, switch to the 5 mm needles. Only knit the 1st row with the smaller size needles. All subsequent repeats are done with the size 5 mm needle).

Row 2: (K1 P2) until 1 st remains. K1 ♠ Repeat from ♠ to ♠ for a total of 6 rows. (*Change colour at the* **START** *of row* **7** *if desired.*)

To save yourself time if you're changing colours, I suggest that you Work in the Ends While Knitting. Scan the QR code below to learn how.

Row 7-11: Knit (*Change colour at the* **START** *of row* **11** *if desired.*)

Row 12 ♦ K1 P2 K1 P8 ♦ Repeat from ♦ to ♦ 2 more times.. K1 P2 K1

Row 13: ♣ K4 C4B C4F ♣ Repeat from ♣ to ♣ 2 more times K4

If you are uncertain how to make the C4B or C4F, you can use the QR codes below:

C4F   C4B

Row 14: ♥ K1 P2 K1 P2 K4 P2 ♥ Repeat from ♥ to ♥ 2 more times. K1 P2 K1

Row 15 K6 ☺ P4 K8 ☺ Repeat from ☺ to ☺ once. P4 K6

Row 16: As row 14

Row 17: As row 15

Row 18: As row 14

Row 19: As row 15

Row 20: As row 14

Row 21: As row 15

Row 22: As row 14

Row 23: ♣ K4 C4B C4F ♣ Repeat from ♣ to ♣ 2 more times K4

Row 24: ♦ K1 P2 K1 P8 ♦ Repeat from ♦ to ♦ 2 more times.. K1 P2 K1

Row 25: Knit

Row 26: As row 24

Row 27: Knit

Row 28: As row 24

Row 29: Knit

Row 30: As row 24

Row 31: ♣ K4 C4B C4F ♣ Repeat from ♣ to ♣ 2 more times K4

Row 32: as row 24 (*Change colour at the **START** of row* **33** *if desired.*)

Row 33 – 36: Knit (*Change colour at the **START** of row* **37** *if desired.*)

▲ ♠ **Row 37:** Knit

Row 38: (K1 P2) until 1 st remains. K1 ♠ Repeat from ♠ to ♠ for a total of **10** rows.

Row 47 - 50: Knit. ▲ Repeat from ▲ to ▲ as many times as you want. ***REMEMBER*** – make it

HALF as long as you want the final scarf. See further suggestions in the *Hints and Tips* section.

When making the last repeat finish with *Row 48*. Cast of on the **RIGHT** side.

Cast off.

Make another half to match.

Sewing the Seam

Sew the seam to join the two halves. When joining leave a length of yarn on one of the halves to use to sew this seam.

When making the seam, pull the sides together so they are snug but not tight. There is a bit of slack naturally between the rows of garter stitch. You want to mimic this as closely as possible.

To join the ends, you'll work between the cast off edge and row 48. You can see in the photo some previously joined stitches. Note where the yarn end is coming out.

With your tapestry needle, pick up the bar that is between the bump of the stitch and the cast off row.

Pull snug.

Pick up the bar that is between the cast off row and the bump of the stitch.

Continue down the length of the seam. It should look like the other garter bands on the scarf. You can

pull the two ends apart a bit to get the stitches to even out the tension along the seam.

Making the Fringe

This is optional. If you are not a fringe person, don't add a fringe. You may prefer a different style of fringe than what I did. Whatever you prefer is perfect.

When you switched from the smaller 4 mm needles to the larger, there became a bend at the end. Along that bend are stitches that run along the bottom. These are perfect for adding the fringe.

I preferred to make the fringe with one strand drawn through. You may want more strands and alternate with every other stitch. There are a lot of fringe tutorials and variations online that you may like more. It's worth taking a look. Regardless, I've provided the instructions to show you how I made my fringe.

Cut lengths of yarn for **twice** the length you want your fringe. Insert your crochet hook in one stitch from the wrong side to the front. Fold one length of yarn in half. Catch with the crochet hook and pull part way through the stitch.

Catch the 2 ends of the yarn and pull through the loop on your hook. Pull the ends snug.

Repeat down the length of the edge.

Hints and Tips

You can use whatever you like for eyes. Buttons will work. I used 8 mm flat back cabochons. They come in a variety of colours and sizes. I looked for more realistic owl eyes but all I could find were ones for taxidermy and they were too big, and expensive. I also recommend gluing them on as sewing will take a bit of time.

Because this is meant to be flat you'll need to block or press it. Use your method of preference. A few tips on pressing - make a test piece to see how your yarn will react and adjust accordingly. I used acrylic yarns for my demo pieces. I made sure my iron was set to a low temperature. I then used a spray bottle to wet it on the WRONG side. I then pressed carefully on the WRONG side. Check the front as you press to make sure it isn't flattening the stitches more than you want.

Your scarf halves don't have to be the same length. If you know there is a particular way you want to wear it, such as very long, wrapped once around your neck and the ends hanging down, you may want the seam on one side instead of the middle, right in the front.

I made my brown scarf as an equal divide. I repeated from ▲ to ▲ 12 times *more* for a total of 13 sections. It's long enough to wrap around my neck and dangle on each side just like in the photo at the start of this publication.

Take a photo of this square for more
FREE knitting patterns on my website!

Knitted Owl Fingerless Gloves

I've made these owl wrist warmers similar to my original knit flat owl half gloves but with this version, they are knit from the fingers to the wrist cuff. The owls are made from feet to head, matching the hat and scarf. There is a slight difference with the appearance of the owls when made from head to feet and I couldn't live with that. Once you see it you can't *not* see it, if you know what I mean.

And since I was doing a redesign, I figured I should make the cuffs match. So I did. I did two versions of the glove. One with a rolled cuff edge (blue and brown) and one without (green). It is clearly marked in the pattern where to stop knitting and cast off depending on the edging you want. And speaking of the final appearance of the granny gloves, there is no reason that these gloves have to match anything. You can also knit them in a single colour. It really is up to you and what look you are after.

To make the thumb gusset blend as much as possible and match on both sides of the thumb, there are different ways to knit and purl the stitches together. It changes whether it is on the left or the right side of the thumb. It is noted how to knit and purl the stitches in the pattern. I've also added links to a helpful how-to video to show you how. You don't have to make the stitches the way I did, but it gives a much better overall look. There's more about this in the *Hints and Tips* section.

If casting on the 13 stitches for the thumb or picking up stitches is confusing for you, there is also a video to help you with that too. The link is after the *Hints and Tips* section.

Things You Need

Worsted weight yarn – 1 standard ball of yarn (215 yards/197 m) will make the gloves in one colour. Any colour combinations of your choosing will work.

Knitting needles:

  Small - Size 3 US (3.25 mm) knitting needles

  Medium - Size 6 US (4 mm) knitting needles

  Large - Size 8 US (5 mm) knitting needles

Tapestry needle - to sew the seam and work in the ends.

4 - 8 mm flat back cabochons or small buttons. You can also embroider eyes on if you prefer.

Gauge

In *stockinette* stitch

Small

size 3.5 mm (US size 4) knitting needles
11 stitches every 2 inches (5 cm)
16 rows every 2 inches (5 cm)

Medium

size 4 mm (US size 6) knitting needles
10 stitches every 2 inches (5 cm)
14 rows every 2 inches (5 cm)

Large

size 5 mm (US size 8) knitting needles
9 stitches every 2 inches (5 cm)
12 rows every 2 inches (5 cm)

Sizing

Like my other fingerless mitt patterns, I've made this as one pattern and adjusted the needle size to change the sizes. This makes it a heck of a lot easier to design and keeps the proportion of the owl the same on all sizes. Frankly, the overall look is better.

To help with the hand sizing, I've included a handy infographic (pun intended). Keep in mind, The gloves will stretch a bit as the stitches relax.

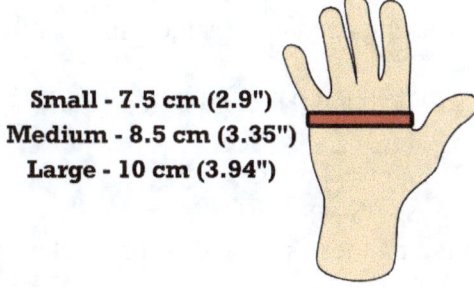

Small - 7.5 cm (2.9")
Medium - 8.5 cm (3.35")
Large - 10 cm (3.94")

Right Hand

Cast on 34 sts

◊ **Row 1:** K across

Row 2: *K1 P2* Repeat from * to * to the last st. K1 ◊ Repeat from ◊ to ◊ for a total of 6 rows.

(*Change colour at the **START** of row **7** if desired.*)

To save yourself time if you're changing colours, I suggest that you Work in the Ends While Knitting. by scanning the QR code below to learn how.

Row 7 – 11: K across (*Change colour at the **START** of row **11** if desired.*)

Row 12: P5 K1 P8 K1 P19

Row 13: K14 Cast on 13 sts K6 C4B C4F K6

If you are uncertain how to make the C4B or C4F, you can use the QR codes below:

Row 14: P5 K1 P2 K4 P2 K1 P32

Row 15: K35 P4 K8

Row 16: P5 K1 P2 K4 P2 K1 P5 P2tog (Slip the next st onto your working needle. Pick up the next st, twist and place back on your non-working needle. Pass the slipped st back onto the non-working needle. Purl the sts together from LEFT to RIGHT). P9 P2tog (Purl these sts together from RIGHT to LEFT – as you normally would). P14

If you need some extra help with making these stitches, you can take a pic of the QR code below:

Row 17: K33 P4 K8

Row 18: P5 K1 P2 K4 P2 K1 P30

Row 19: K14 K2tog (Knit the sts together from LEFT to RIGHT). K7 K2tog (Pick up the next st, twist and place back on your non-working needle. Knit the 2 sts together from RIGHT to LEFT) K8 P4 K8

This is the same video as above but starts at the how to K2tog section.

Row 20: P5 K1 P2 K4 P2 K1 P28

Row 21: K31 P4 K8

Row 22: P5 K1 P2 K4 P2 K1 P5 P2tog (as before – pass the next st over, pick up and twist next st, pass slipped st back. Purl from left to right) P5 P2tog (P right to left) P14.

Row 23: K27 C4B C4F K6

Row 24: P5 K1 P8 K1 P26

Row 25: K14 K2tog (from left to right) K3 K2tog (as before – pick up next st, twist, knit from right to left). K20

Row 26: P5 K1 P8 K1 P24

Row 27: K across

Row 28: P5 K1 P8 K1 P5 P2tog (as before – pass the next st over, pick up and twist next st, pass slipped st back. Purl from left to right) P1 P2tog (P right to left). P14

Row 29: K across

Row 30: P5 K1 P8 K1 P22

Row 31: K14 K3tog (from left to right) K6 C4B C4F K6

Row 32: P5 K1 P8 K1 P20

(*Change colour at the **START** of row **33** if desired.*)

Row 33 – 37: K across. (*Change colour at the **START** of row **37** if desired.*)

Row 38: K2tog. ♠ P2 K1 ♠ Repeat from ♠ to ♠ to the end of the row.

☺ **Row39:** K across

Row 40: ♦ K1 P2 ♦ Repeat from ♦ to ♦ to the last st. K1 ☺ Repeat from ☺ to ☺ for a total of 10 rows.

Continue with the rest of the pattern if you would like a rolled edge to match the edging of the owl beanie hat. If you don't like the rolled edge, cast off. Leave a longer length of yarn to sew the seam.

◘ **Row 49:** K across

Row 50: P across. ◘ Repeat from ◘ to ◘ for a total of 8 rows.

Cast off. Leave a longer length of yarn to sew the seam.

Thumb

With the RIGHT side of the glove facing you, pick up the 13 sts you cast on in row 13.

Row 1 – 4: K across (*Change colour at the START of row 4 of the thumb if desired.*)

Row 5: ♦ K1 P2 ♦ Repeat from ♦ to ♦ to the last st. K1

Row 6: K across

Row 7: ♦ K1 P2 ♦ Repeat from ♦ to ♦ to the last st. K1

Cast off. Leave a length of yarn to sew the thumb seam.

Left Hand

Cast on 34 sts

◊ **Row 1:** K across

Row 2: *K1 P2* Repeat from * to * to the last st. K1 ◊ Repeat from ◊ to ◊ for a total of 6 rows.

(*Change colour at the START of row 7 if desired.*)

Row 7 – 11: K across (*Change colour at the START of row 11 if desired.*)

Row 12: P19 K1 P8 K1 P5

Row 13: K6 C4B C4F K6 Cast on 13 sts K14

Row 14: P32 K1 P2 K4 P2 K1 P5

Row 15: K8 P4 K35

Row 16: P14 P2tog (Slip the next st onto your working needle. Pick up the next st, twist and place back on your non-working needle. Pass the slipped st back onto the non-working needle. Purl the sts together from LEFT to RIGHT). P9 P2tog (Purl these sts together from RIGHT to LEFT – as you normally would). P5 K1 P2 K4 P2 K1 P5

Row 17: K8 P4 K33

Row 18: P30 K1 P2 K4 P2 K1 P5

Row 19: K8 P4 K8 K2tog (Knit the sts together from LEFT to RIGHT). K7 K2tog (Pick up the next st, twist and place back on your non-working needle. Knit the 2 sts together from RIGHT to LEFT) K14

Row 20: P28 K1 P2 K4 P2 K1 P5

Row 21: K8 P4 K31

Row 22: P14 P2tog (as before – pass the next st over, pick up and twist next st, pass slipped st back.

Purl from left to right) P5 P2tog (P right to left) P5 K1 P2 K4 P2 K1 P5

Row 23: K6 C4B C4F K27

Row 24: P26 K1 P8 K1 P5

Row 25: K20 K2tog (from left to right) K3 K2tog (as before – pick up next st, twist, knit from right to

left). K14

Row 26: P24 K1 P8 K1 P5

Row 27: K across

Row 28: P14 P2tog (as before – pass the next st over, pick up and twist next st, pass slipped st back.

Purl from left to right) P1 P2tog (P right to left). P5 K1 P8 K1 P5

Row 29: K across

Row 30: P22 K1 P8 K1 P5

Row 31: K6 C4B C4F K6 K3tog (from left to right) K14

Row 32: P20 K1 P8 K1 P5

*(Change colour at the **START** of row 33 if desired.)*

Row 33 – 37: K across. *(Change colour at the **START** of row 37 if desired.)*

Row 38: K2tog. ♠ P2 K1 ♠ Repeat from ♠ to ♠ to the end of the row.

☺ **Row39:** K across

Row 40: ♦ K1 P2 ♦ Repeat from ♦ to ♦ to the last st. K1 ☺ Repeat from ☺ to ☺ for a total of 10 rows.

Continue with the rest of the pattern if you would like a rolled edge to match the edging of the owl

beanie hat. If you don't like the rolled edge, cast off. Leave a longer length of yarn to sew the seam.

◘ **Row 49:** K across

Row 50: P across. ◘ Repeat from ◘ to ◘ for a total of 8 rows.

Cast off. Leave a longer length of yarn to sew the seam

Thumb

With the RIGHT side of the glove facing you, pick up the 13 sts you cast on in row 13.

Row 1 – 4: K across (*Change colour at the **START** of row **4 of the thumb** if desired.*)

Row 5: ♦ K1 P2 ♦ Repeat from ♦ to ♦ to the last st. K1

Row 6: K across

Row 7: ♦ K1 P2 ♦ Repeat from ♦ to ♦ to the last st. K1

Cast off. Leave a length of yarn to sew the thumb seam.

Hints and Tips

If you don't P2tog and K2tog as indicated in the pattern, you'll end up with one very defined line on one side of the thumb gusset, and a much less refined edge on the other. I tried many combos to make the side of the gusset match. Making the stitches as indicated in the pattern allow for this.

This photo is what the thumb gusset will look like if you knit and purl the stitches without following the instructions.

You don't need to add the extra garter and ribbing for the thumb. It is a finished edge so it won't come undone. You may want to do a quick single crochet around to give it a bit of a fancy edging.

You can use whatever you like for eyes. Buttons will work. I used 8 mm flat back cabochons. They come in a variety of colours and sizes. I looked for more realistic owl eyes but all I could find were ones for taxidermy and they were too big, and expensive. I also recommend gluing them on as sewing will take a bit of time.

Watch the Helpful Thumb Video

If you need help with casting on the thumb or picking up the stitches to finish the thumb, you can watch the quick how-to video on Youtube here - Basic Fingerless Gloves - How to Make the Thumb

You can also take a pic of the QR code below. When you take a photo, a link will pop up on your phone or tablet. Tap the link and the video will automatically start to play. The video is for a different fingerless glove style, but is a very similar technique.

Abbreviations

K - knit

P - purl

K2tog - knit 2 sts together

P2tog - purl 2 together

K3tog - knit 3 stitches together

st - stitch

sts – stitches

Side note: I use both versions of the terminology when it comes to cable stitches. I've been corrected that I'm using the wrong one for both occasions so it's a no win for me. What I mean is that C4F is the same technique as C2F. Just like how C2B is the same as C4B. Do you think of it as the just the stitches you're pulling or the number of stitches you're using in total when you do it? It's a personal choice, I guess.

C4F - Pick up the next 2 stitches with your cable needle. Pull the stitches to the FRONT of your work. Knit the next 2 stitches on your non-working needle. Knit the 2 stitches from the cable needle. Watch this video to see how. How to C4F or Cable 4 Forward.

C4B - Pick up the next 2 stitches with your cable needle. Pull the stitches to the BACK of your work. Knit the next 2 stitches on your non-working needle. Knit the 2 stitches from the cable needle. Watch this video to see how. How to C4B or Cable 4 Back

Like all of my patterns, you have my permission to sell and/or give away the physical items that you make using this pattern. You are NOT permitted to reprint this pattern in any form unless you have obtained my written permission to do so.

If you have any questions, please feel free to leave a comment or send me your questions at kweenbee_crafts@hotmail.ca.

Help Support My Work!

Follow me on Instagram, Facebook, Pinterest and YouTube. Every follow, subscribe, thumbs up, like, heart and share help increase my popularity on the web and get more viewers to my work. It costs you nothing but helps me sooooo much!

If you would like to help a little more, you can always become a Website Member to download print over 45 patterns. Or you can support me by becoming a Patron on Patreon or you can make a single time donation at Buy Me a Coffee.

You can use any of these QR codes to find out more.

Website Member

Patreon

Buy Me a Coffee

More FREE knitting patterns on my website

I'm always creating new patterns and I post every one of them over on my website. It is an ever growing list so you might want to check out my **Free Knitting Patterns** page at **KweenBee.com** . I design new patterns as I get time. I aim to add a couple new ones each month so the list is always growing!

Here are a few of the most popular knitting patterns you may enjoy. You can click the link or the pic to see the pattern in full on my website.

Autumn Leaf Half Gloves

Ribbed Moccasin Bootie Slippers for Adults

Diamonds Dishcloth

Winter Beanie Toque or Touque or Tuque with Vertical Stripes

Ultra Thick Slip-On Bootie Slippers

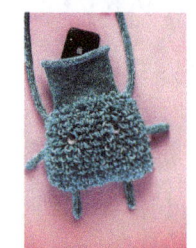
How to Knit a Way Cool Monster Purse

Minimalist Round Toe Slippers

How to Knit a Pair of Flip Mittens or Fingerless Gloves

Of course, none of the links will work. To make it even easier, you can take a photo of the QR code below with your phone or tablet. A link will pop up. Tap that link and it will take you right to the webpage to see all of the patterns above and even more!

You can also do a search for the titles online if QR codes are something that you feel you are unable or don't want to use it.

When you are on your favourite search engine like Google, Bing, Yahoo, etc. Enter the term *Kweenbee* and the title as it is written below (capitalization isn't important). It will pop up for you in the search results and be super-easy to find.

For example, enter it like this:

Google

kweenbee Diamonds Dishcloth

Google Search   I'm Feeling Lucky

Google offered in: Français

Your results will have my pattern at the very top...usually. Depending on the popularity of the pattern, you may get a link to Pinterest or Ravelry first. Don't worry! All of those options have links back to my original patterns, too!

This is only a partial list btw. The full list is much longer, running nearly 2 pages.

Easy to Knit Basic Fingerless Gloves

Basic Knit Flat Beanie or Toque

Hippo Fingerless Gloves

Cozy Cuff Slippers

Bulky Yarn Slippers on Straight Needles – Knit Flat on 2 Needles

How to Knit Spider Fingerless Gloves - Knit Flat on 2 Needles

One Piece Knitted Dishcloth and Coasters

Easy to Knit Long Cuffed Slippers

Easy to Knit Rolled Cuff Slippers

Knit a Pair of Texting Mitts

Chevron Striped Moccasin Slippers

Super Cozy Textured Adult Bootie Slippers

Textured Easy to Knit Dishcloth Pattern

Super Simple Fingerless Gloves – Knit Flat on 2 Needles

Knit Long Fingerless Gloves – Two Styles with One Pattern

Super Simple Knit Slippers

Follow Me on Social Media

Take a photo with your phone or tablet of the QR codes below. A link will appear. Click the link to go straight to my social media page.

Twitter　　　　YouTube　　　　Threads

Facebook　　　　Instagram　　　　Pinterest

Patreon　　　　My Etsy Shop　　　　Buy Me a Coffee

www.ingramcontent.com/pod-product-compliance
Lightning Source LLC
Chambersburg PA
CBHW081011120626
46546CB00010B/3104